Contents

Words in bold letters **like these** are explained in the Glossary.

Dance and you

To dance, you need a body you can move!

Wear light, comfortable clothes, so that you can move easily.

shoulder

head

arm

hand

bottom

leg

foot

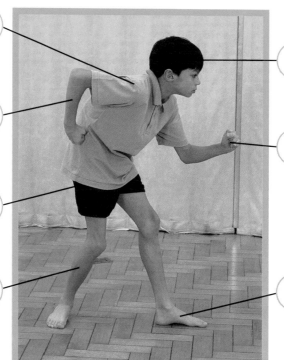

You will need some music, too.

YOU CAN DO IT!

Dance

Barry Gibson

Heinemann
LIBRARY

First published in Great Britain by Heinemann Library
Halley Court, Jordan Hill, Oxford OX2 8EJ
a division of Reed Educational and Professional Publishing Ltd.
Heinemann is a registered trademark of Reed Educational & Professional Publishing Limited.

OXFORD MELBOURNE AUCKLAND IBADAN JOHANNESBURG
BLANTYRE GABORONE PORTSMOUTH (NH) USA CHICAGO

Designed by Ken Vail Graphic Design, Cambridge
Illustrations by Graham-Cameron Illustration (Sarah Hedley)
Originated by Ambassador Litho Ltd
Printed by Wing King Tong in Hong Kong

04 03 02 01 00
10 9 8 7 6 5 4 3 2 1

ISBN 0 431 08538 2

British Library Cataloguing in Publication Data

Gibson, Barry
Dance. – (You can do it)
1. Dance – Juvenile literature
I. Title
792.8

Acknowledgements
The Publishers would like to thank Jaqui Isow and the pupils of Bishops Stortford School of
Performing Arts for all their help in the preparation of this book.

The Publishers would like to thank the following for permission to reproduce photographs:
Trevor Clifford, pages 4, 5, 6, 8, 10, 19, 22; Dee Conway, pages 14, 16, 17 (top and bottom),
20 (bottom); Corbis, page 12; Performing Arts, page 20 (top).

Cover photograph reproduced with permission of Collections/Anthea Sieveking

Our thanks to Betty Root for her comments in the preparation of this book.

Every effort has been made to contact copyright holders of any material reproduced in this book.
Any omissions will be rectified in subsequent printings if notice is given to the Publisher.

For more information about Heinemann Library books, or to order, please phone 01865 888066,
or send a fax to 01865 314091. You can visit our web site at www.heinemann.co.uk

You can begin by walking in different ways.
Try being strong and heavy, then gentle
and light.

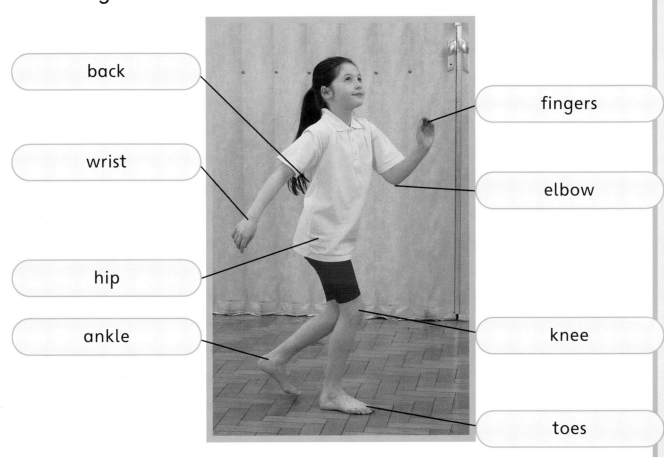

back

wrist

hip

ankle

fingers

elbow

knee

toes

Are you ready?

Before you do any dance, make sure your body is ready. This is called a **warm-up**. You need to warm up all the different parts of your body, especially your **muscles**.

Start by bending, swinging or **stretching**.

SAFETY STAR

Always warm up your body before you dance, so that you don't hurt yourself.

Try doing these things to warm up your whole body!

Touch your toes.

Stretch up high.

Wiggle your fingers.

Wiggle your toes.

Wiggle your elbows.

Wiggle your nose.

Shake your shoulders.

Roll your head.

Swing from side to side.

Turn right round.

Walk on the spot.

Run on the spot.

Breathe deep and rest. Now, let's move!

Let's move!

Here are some different ways to walk.

| Stepping with your heels. | Stepping with the sides of your feet. | Stepping on tiptoe. |

Our bodies can leap, hop, skip and jump, a bit like animals moving.

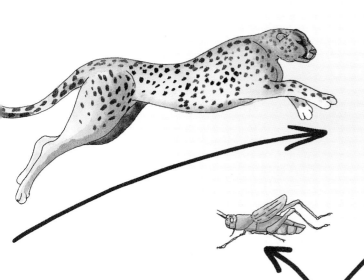

There are lots of ways to turn and twist your body round.

Can you spin and twist like this?

Which way shall we go?

You can move yourself in different **directions**.

Try going forwards, backwards and sideways.

These children are rising high up in the air and sinking low down to the ground.

Imagine you are looking down at yourself from the ceiling.

Here are some floor patterns to try.

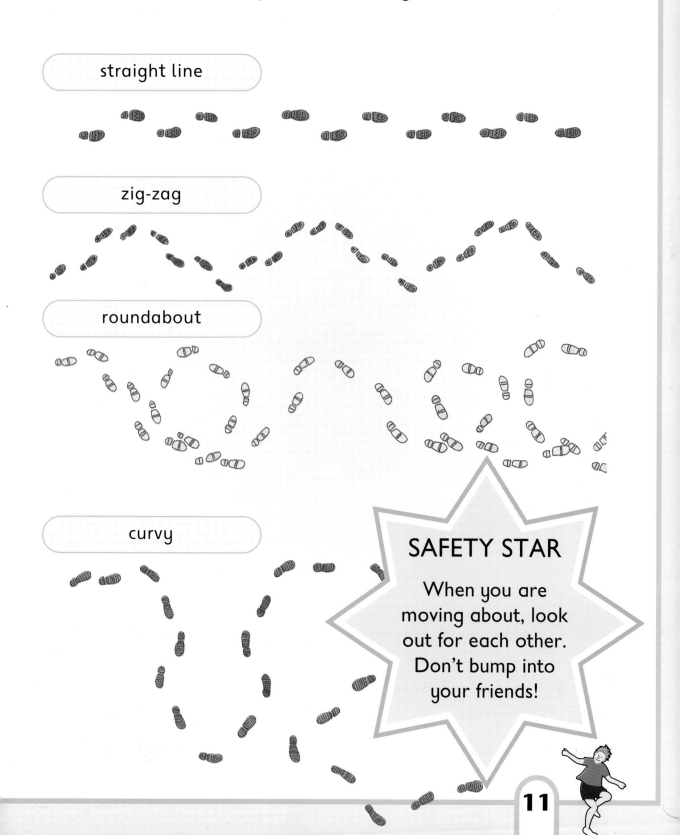

straight line

zig-zag

roundabout

curvy

SAFETY STAR

When you are moving about, look out for each other. Don't bump into your friends!

Move together

In a dance space, a group of people can make all sorts of shapes together.

There are lines, rows, squares and circles.

This is a circle dance from Bulgaria. It is performed at the Festival of Roses.

It is also fun to work with a friend.

You can meet each other...   ...and then you can part.

You can make an
arch together.

You can gently push and
pull each other, without
falling over.

SAFETY STAR

Help your partner
to balance safely.
Support them
well.

Step in time

Dance and music go together well.

Some dances are fast.

Here is a Kathak dancer from India. In parts of the dance her feet tap the floor very quickly.

Some dances are slow and steady.

This dance is called a Pavane. It was first danced about 400 years ago.

People thought the smooth, proud movements were like a peacock.

Rhythm is the way music and sounds make patterns in time. In dance music, the rhythm helps you know when to move.

Sometimes the music has a strong **beat**.

Here are some actions to try in time to some music.

walk

jog

tiptoe

bounce

hop

freeze

Feel the rhythm in your feet!

What's the idea?

Dance is also a way of sharing ideas with an **audience**. A dance might create a **mood**. It may make the audience feel happy or sad. It might tell a story.

Dances from a particular time or place are often in a special **style**.

What words might describe the style of this dance?

Each style of dance needs a different kind of dance **energy**. Sometimes a style has special **steps**.

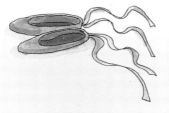

For some kinds of dance the dancers wear special shoes.

Who am I?

Have you ever wanted to be someone or something else?

By moving in special ways, you can become a different **character** in an instant!

Which movements and **gestures** might you make for these characters?

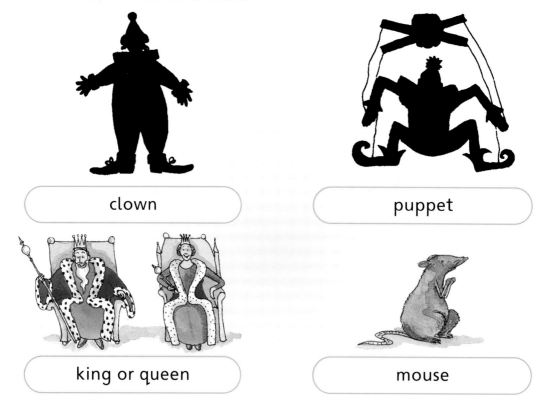

clown

puppet

king or queen

mouse

Are they scared? Happy? Sad? Cross?

Perhaps the dance might show how the characters change their **mood**. You could put some of your dance ideas together to make a story in dance.

This group of friends has joined up to make a crazy machine together.

Each person is making a different movement.

SAFETY STAR
In a group dance, avoid bumps and falls. If you are holding or leaning against each other, do so carefully!

Keep your eyes open!

When doing a show, dancers sometimes wear special **costumes**.

They may also use special **props**. These are objects which help make the **performance** seem real.

Can you make up a dance with a chair?

SAFETY STAR

Check props are safe to use. Make sure you don't fall off or over them!

To make sense, every dance needs a beginning, a middle and an end.

Movements put together can make a **sequence**.

Some dance **styles** have special sequences called **routines**.

Here is part of a rock'n'roll routine. The steps are very lively.

A **choreographer** decides which movements make up a dance.

Can you plan some movements and actions for a group of friends?

Cool it!

After using lots of **energy**, you need to let your body calm down.

After all that work, you might feel stiff.

Your arms and legs might ache a little.

You might feel hot. So, cool it!

SAFETY STAR

Remember to **cool down** after dancing, so that your body can go back to normal, slowly and easily.

Here is one way to cool down.

1 Stand still and close your eyes.

2 Breathe with slow, deep breaths.

3 Now lie on your back.

4 Let your whole body sink into the floor.

5 Relax your head. Let it go loose.

6 Relax your shoulders.

7 Relax your arms.

8 Relax your fingers.

9 Relax your back.

10 Relax your legs.

11 Relax your toes.

12 Take your time to open your eyes.

Glossary

audience people watching a performance

beat sound that comes again and again

character people or creatures

choreographer someone who chooses or plans the movements that make up a dance

cool-down relaxing your muscles after dancing or exercise

costume special clothes worn during a show or performance

direction where you want your body to go

energy power inside you that helps you to move

gesture special action or sign, with your body or your face

mood how people are feeling or thinking

muscle part of your body which helps you bend and stretch

performance special event where you dance for other people

prop object used in a show to make the performance more real, such as a table or chair

routine sequence of dance steps that you learn

rhythm pattern of sounds in time

sequence movements in a special order

steps movements with your feet

stretching moving your muscles as much as you can

style way of dancing, perhaps from a particular time or place

warm-up getting your body and muscles ready for exercise

Index